I Hate Writing

I Hate Writing

◆

The Unofficial Guide to Freshman Composition and Undergraduate Writing

J. M. Bohannon

iUniverse, Inc.
New York Lincoln Shanghai

I Hate Writing
The Unofficial Guide to Freshman Composition and Undergraduate Writing

Copyright © 2005 by J.M. Bohannon

All rights reserved. No part of this book may be used or reproduced by any means, graphic, electronic, or mechanical, including photocopying, recording, taping or by any information storage retrieval system without the written permission of the publisher except in the case of brief quotations embodied in critical articles and reviews.

iUniverse books may be ordered through booksellers or by contacting:

iUniverse
2021 Pine Lake Road, Suite 100
Lincoln, NE 68512
www.iuniverse.com
1-800-Authors (1-800-288-4677)

ISBN: 0-595-34943-9

Printed in the United States of America

Contents

INTRODUCTION vii
CHAPTER 1 A RIVER OF ENGLISH 1
CHAPTER 2 IMAGE OF A WRITER 7
CHAPTER 3 TB—PREVENTION AND TREATMENT 11
CHAPTER 4 THE STRAIGHT AND NARROW 15
CHAPTER 5 THE CLAY 17
CHAPTER 6 LISTENING TO THE PAGE 20
CHAPTER 7 SAYING HELLO 25
CHAPTER 8 A NOTE ON THE FRIDGE 28
CHAPTER 9 STAGES OF REVISION 33
CHAPTER 10 THE PINK TUMMY OF WRITING 40
CHAPTER 11 IT TAKES ALL KINDS 45
CHAPTER 12 PERSUASIVE AWARENESS 51
CHAPTER 13 THE RESEARCH PAPER 56
CONCLUSION: I HATE WRITING 61

INTRODUCTION

Follow the accident, fear the fixed plan—that is the rule.

—John Fowles

I was having dinner with a group of professors at a Hemingway conference not long ago. We were introducing ourselves and doing all that "intro" talk that people who don't know each other (and don't know if they even want to know each other) do. The wave of conversation eventually moved to me.

"What is your specialty, Miss Bohannon?" The bearded man placed his emphasis on <u>Miss</u>. I was the only person at the table without a Ph.D. in hand.

"I teach writing."

"Creative?" the professor asked.

"No. I teach composition."

"Oh," he replied with distaste, raising his eyebrows apologetically before turning to join another conversation.

A few minutes later, he turned his attention back to me. "Don't worry," he said, "I still have to teach a comp. class every semester, and I've been with the university for over five years."

I tried to explain that I *enjoyed* teaching composition, that I *wanted* to teach composition, that the *only subject I wanted to teach* was composition. I don't think he believed me. I wasn't surprised.

Teaching composition in many universities is the equivalent of grunt work. It is, in a sense, what professional academics in the field of English consider "paying your dues." Too often, composition is even taught with "initiation" mentality: this was done to me, so now I do it to you. Thankfully, things are changing, (and in many places have been changing for some time), but too many composition courses are still taught by fledgling professors and graduate students who like teaching composition about as much as they like eating dirt.

There are progressive composition instructors out there, and they are growing in number. They want students to cultivate their writing, to understand that writing is a way to learn and a way to discover. They emphasize the process of writing (from the seed of an idea, through the planting and nurturing, all the way to harvest) and encourage their students to revel in their mistakes, to embrace their errors, and to celebrate writing.

You could probably poll English professors from all over the U.S. and the number of those professors who actually enjoyed the composition classes they had to take as freshmen would be very low. I wonder how many professors would confess that they actually did not learn very much from those classes, let alone anything about writing. I certainly didn't.

The fact is, what writing instructors teach and what they do in their own writing is radically different. Pick up any scholarly journal and the chances of your coming across a nice five-paragraph essay are slim. In fact, the day you find the type of writing that some comp. instructors teach in the professional world of academia will be the day your pet fish asks to borrow your car keys.

Why do instructors tell students one thing and do another? Because teaching writing is difficult. Quite frankly, it is impossible to teach someone to write. Can you teach someone to ride a bike? Think about it. You can show someone how *you* ride a bike, but people have to learn to balance on their own. They have to get their own scratched elbows and knees. The problem with teaching writing is that, unlike math or chemistry, there really is no set method to learn good writing. By trying to impose an unbending structure to writing, all we really do is kill creativity and invention. At some point the training wheels have to come off.

What makes teaching writing even more difficult is that nobody ever learns to write and that's that. It's not like learning that $2 + 2 = 4$. Writing is a continuing process that changes as we change, that grows as we grow, that matures as we mature. It continues to move through unending cycles of metamorphosis throughout our entire lives. And the more we write, the more our writing changes. The worst thing we can do to our writing is try to keep it from changing, to shackle it until it becomes monotonous and hopelessly patterned.

I know for many of you these are not things you want to hear. "Just give us the formula, pleeeeeease!" one of my students pleaded last year. "All this process and revision crap just makes writing confusing and difficult." Well, there's truth to that statement. Real writing (as opposed to the pseudo-writing known as the five-paragraph essay) isn't easy. Real writing means investing your time, your emotions, your mind, your whole self into what you are writing. Real writing—true writing—has no formula.

So how does one (me, for instance), considering that it's impossible to teach writing, teach a student to write a good paper in four months, in the brevity of a semester? The answer is simple (at least relatively simple). I give students freedom. Peter Elbow, one of the forefathers of composition theory and Director of the writing program at the University of Massachusetts—Amherst, says "We can trust students; we don't have to do everything for them." Part of trusting students is allowing them to find their own strengths in writing and giving them space to learn, space for change. Teaching with freedom, however, cannot be one-sided. I will trust you to learn to write. You must trust yourself to become a writer.

◆   ◆   ◆

Fast Forward.

◆   ◆   ◆

I no longer teach composition. After giving birth to twin boys who possess more energy than space shuttle at lift-off, I have relegated myself to home base. I have pened my own editing company, and now I try to show my clients ways to edit their own work instead of relying on another's sharp eye. But I wanted future students to have access to a textbook on writing that would not put them to sleep before they finished the first paragraph, a textbook that would help them become writers. So I have put my book on the market as the Unofficial Guide to Freshman Composition and Undergraduate Writing.

If you have purchased this text (or borrowed it from a friend), I hope you enjoy the following pages. But be warned. I will ask you to question everything you may have been taught about writing. However, in the same way that I want you to question what you have learned in the past, I expect you to question everything I write in this text. I want you to realize, right now, that simply because something is published does not mean that it is "right" or the only way of seeing things. Use your head, evaluate the evidence, and go with your instincts. Always be willing to listen to someone else's opinion, but know when to stand up for your own. Above all, have faith in yourself.

1

A RIVER OF ENGLISH

Spoken words are the symbols of mental experience and written words are the symbols of spoken words.

—Aristotle (On Interpretation)

What exactly is English? The language you speak? The words you use to write? The class you hate or love in school? Have you ever asked yourself how the language we call English came into being? Especially for people who think they can't write or who don't like English courses because they hate grammar, a little information about the history of this dreaded language might put things in perspective.

As you are probably well aware, there are endless rules of grammar. But where did these rules come from? Did man, while he was out hunting (or woman), suddenly stumble upon a number of large, engraved stones that explained the English language and say, "Oh! So that's how we're supposed to write and speak English!" Well, no. Of course not. It might surprise you to know that we've only had set rules for English grammar for the last 200 years, which, considering we can trace English back nearly 1,500 years, is a relatively short time.

The historical development of English is quite interesting (especially to us linguist freaks), but an in-depth study is not the aim of this text. For those who are interested in a detailed history, there are a number of books on the subject. I recommend <u>A History of the English Language</u> by Baugh and Cable. My aim is simply to provide you with a brief overview of the changes English has gone through to give you a broader view of the language you speak and write and the rules you have been taught. Here we go.

Linguists have traced the ancestry of most European and Indian languages to a common ancestor, or parent language, which they call Indo-European. There is no actual record of such a language, but linguistic studies have hypothesized a unified beginning by tracing the early sound traits these languages share. The following chart from Stanley Hussey's <u>The English Language: Structure and Development</u> shows the many languages linked to those Indo-European roots.

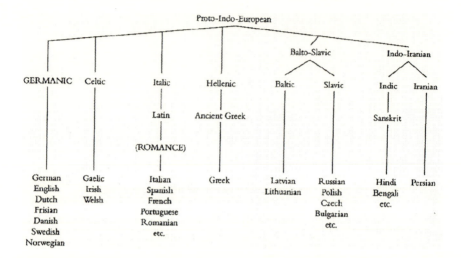

Around 450, Germanic tribes known as the Jutes, Saxons, and Angles invaded the land we know as England. After a time, the three tribes were simply referred to as Angles. *English* derived from *Engle*, which came from *Angle*. What we consider Old English developed from the distinct dialects of the three tribes. Linguists consider the years between 450 and 1150 the Old English stage of our language.

Old English grammar is similar to that of modern German. The nouns in Old English have different endings (inflections) depending on their number (singular or plural) and their case (their purpose in a sentence as a subject, possessive, direct object, or indirect object). Adjectives were spelled differently depending on whether or not you used an article (a, an, the, that, those), and words were classified by gender (masculine, feminine, neuter). Only the verb structure of Old English resembles that of Modern English. Consider the following section from the <u>The Nativity according to Luke</u>, translated here into Old English. The words hardly seem related to the English we know.

> Soþlice on þam dagum wæs geworden gebod fram þam casereAugusto, þæt eall ymbehwyrft wære tomearcod. Þeos tomearcodneswæs æryst geworden fram þam deman Syrige Cirino. And ealle hig eodon,and syndrige ferdon on hyra ceastre. (translator unknown)

The Normans, Scandinavians who had assimilated French language and culture, conquered England in 1066 (The Norman Conquest). For the next 200 years, French was the language of both the ruling class and the upper class, but the majority (the peasants) still spoke English. English adopted French words by the thousands, and Old English began to change.

By 1150, English had shifted to what we know as Middle English, the language of Chaucer. The different endings for nouns, the use of grammatical gender, and the distinctive forms of pronouns, articles, and adjectives dropped out of the language. France conquered Normandy in 1204, releasing the Norman ties in England, and English once again took its place as the primary language. Consider the same section from The Nativity According to Luke translated into Middle English. Now the words begin to resemble the English we use today.

> And it was don in tho daies, a maundement wente out fro the emperour August, that al the world schulde be discryued. This firste discryuyng was maad of Cyryn, iustice of Sirie. And alle men wenten to make professioun, ech in to his owne citee. (translation by John Wycliffe, c. 1380–83)

The men who transcribed the literary works during this time spelled words as they saw fit, so numerous spellings for the same words existed. In 1476 William Caxton introduced the printing press to England. The increased output of written material this invention made possible unintentionally fixed English spellings. In other words, if one spelling was printed more than another, that spelling became the standard. Two or more spellings of many words still existed during this time, however.

Between 1350 and 1550, a sound shift occurred known as the Great Vowel Shift, which altered the pronunciation of English dramatically. The final e of words became silent, and the vowels shifted slightly in pronunciation. Name, for instance, went from <nô mā> (nAH mAY) to <nām> (nAYm). The modern spelling of English words, for this reason, does not necessarily signify the pronunciation of those words, as it does in languages such as Spanish. Here is the same passage from The Nativity According to Luke, this time in Modern English.

> And it came to pass in those days, that there went out a decree from Caesar Augustus that all the world should be taxed. (And this taxing was first made when Cyrenius was governor of Syria.) and all went to be taxed, every one into his own city. (King James Version, 1604)

By the mid-to-late 1600s, writers began to desire further standardization of spellings (one spelling, not three) as well as a written analysis of English grammar.

It's not hard to understand the reasons people wanted and perhaps needed to set grammatical standards for English. Imagine that a new game has evolved from an American sport, and everyone enjoys playing it, but everyone plays it a little differently. There are no rules. Eventually, after people struggle to play without rules long enough, they realize they need to decide what the rules should be, so there will be no confusion over certain plays and so their game can become, lets say, an Olympic sport.

In the late 17th and early 18th centuries, English was that sport. People were writing, but there were no rules to govern that writing. The Spanish had possessed a written "grammar" dating from 1492. The French had established a literary academy, the Académie Française, in 1634 to set standards for, ensure purity of, and limit change to their language. English speakers did not want to be left out. They wanted their language to have the recognition and respect of other countries, and they wanted English to be on par with the "professional" language of use, Latin. (It is important to note that writing in English was considered vulgar and uneducated). In 1662, and again in 1712, The Royal Society of London attempted to create an academy to govern and improve the English language. Both attempts failed.

Samuel Johnson, addressing both the demand and need of the time, published the first English dictionary in 1755. Robert Lowth, following suit, published his *Short Introduction to English Grammar* in 1762. Studies in grammar quickly gained interest, and numbers of books on grammar began to come into print. However, "most of these books were the work of men with no special qualifications for the thing they attempted to do" (Baugh 271). Those self-made grammarians made decisions about correctness that are still with us today. Lie and Lay, for instance, did not possess distinct conjugations before this time, and students continue to have problems distinguishing between the two.

Throughout the remainder of the 17th century and on into the 18th century, grammarians increased in number and became forceful and uncompromising. They thought of themselves as grammar gods who had the authority to declare what was or was not correct usage. They moved from descriptive practices—observing the natural, internal grammatical rules of a language that explain how people speak—to prescriptive practices—declaring how people should speak.

Today, modern linguists "understand their job as that of description, their purpose being to *de*scribe how people actually use language, not to *pre*scribe how they *should* use it" (Kolln, 4). Years of reliance on prescriptive grammar, however, has hardened many grammarians and English teachers so that they refuse to acknowledge any form of change. But whether or not we like or accept the evolution of our language, that evolution will continue. Language is alive, and like all living things, its nature is change. Consider the following observations of present-day English:

- Splitting infinitives (now approved by the Oxford English Dictionary)

    Correct: I want you to evaluate critically the text.
    Considered Incorrect Until Recently: I want you to critically evaluate the text.

- Dropping the subjunctive mood

    Correct: I wish I were going with him.
    Incorrect: I wish I was going with him.

- Using which to refer to an idea instead of a specific word

    Correct: Studying grammar, an activity which isn't always fun, is important.
    Incorrect: Studying grammar, which isn't always fun, is important

- Using their to eliminate sexism

    Correct: Every student should bring a copy of his or her manual.
    Incorrect: Every student should bring a copy of their manual.

- Dropping the—ly of some adverbs

    Correct: Come quickly!
    Incorrect: Come quick!

In the years to come, the above usages may eventually gain approval from the necessary *authorities*. But perhaps they never will. In any case, I want you to understand that WE make the rules of our language. The way we speak, the way we write, and the way we use our language determine the rules of our language—not the other way around.

However, understanding the rules of grammar is important. For right or wrong, your command of the English language in both speech and writing (meaning your adherence to prescribed grammatical rules) will affect the way people (especially employers and professors) perceive you. Knowledge of grammar is the only weapon you can use to fight prescribed forms.

For now, I want you to use this history lesson for your benefit. The English of yesterday is not the English of today, and the English of today will not be the English of tomorrow. So write with a sense of freedom. There's no perfect paper in the sky that you must compare with everything you write. There's only you, your ideas, your words, and your desire to communicate. Heraclitus, an early Greek philosopher once said, "One never steps in the same river twice." Think of English as a river. But don't just get your feet wet. Plunge in, brave the cold, and go with the flow.

2
IMAGE OF A WRITER

The most difficult task for a writer is to get the right "voice" for his material; by voice I mean the overall impression one has of the creator behind what he creates.

—*John Fowles*

You have most likely been taught to write in a certain way, in a certain format, perhaps even told where each sentence should go. Now it is time to become a writer. The point of your writing should no longer be to fit into some prescribed form. The point of your writing should be to communicate. Give yourself the freedom to break out and find your own style. Your individuality as a writer should shine through. This is probably the hardest thing to do, something you may spend a lifetime working on. When you discover your individuality as a writer, you will find your voice.

Probably the most important aspect of good writing is voice. What is voice? Voice is a way of speaking. Actors like Melanie Griffith, Tom Cruise, Christopher Walken, Sandra Bullock and Samuel L. Jackson have unique ways of speaking and unique mannerisms that accompany their speech. These characteristics make up each actor's individual voice. Each one of us, in the same way, has a distinctive way of speaking that we develop from the moment we start forming words—perhaps even before.

Your unique voice should blast through your writing, letting all who read what you write know there's a person behind your words. Too many students approach writing at the university level as a scientist approaches a volatile experiment: with protective suit, goggles, gloves, and forceps. They struggle to write without contaminating that writing with anything resembling personality. Wendy Bishop, professor of English at Florida State University and a prolific author of books about writing, explains that a student can try "so hard to sound academic that 'there's nobody home,' no authentic voice left, no sense of a real human being trying to say something to somebody" (175). Don't let that student be you.

Sometimes it's hard to distinguish your unique voice in writing when you feel you don't have anything to say. The majority of university papers are designed to train you to write, to teach you information, and to prepare you for further work in a certain field. Although the purpose of such writing is good, actually doing it can be a bit dull, and the product may not reflect the passion you have for your interests or your future. A student, for instance, may want to be a doctor, but that does not necessarily mean that he or she is going to be invigorated by writing a paper about the bonding of carbon molecules.

Usually it takes experience (personal and academic) for us to form and transform ideas that we feel strongly about—ideas that compel us to write. Some of you may have subjects of popular interest that you are itching to write about, anxious to throw your opinion into the conversation soup of controversy. On the other hand, some of you may not have found the same passion. That's fine. You don't have to push yourself into the public arena to write. And you should never feel that you have nothing to say simply because the subjects you are interested in are not plastered on the evening news. I believe we all have something to contribute. If you take the time to look inside your hearts and your minds, you might just find the voice you never knew was there.

Becoming a writer and finding your voice takes more than jotting down words on paper and handing them in for a grade. Becoming a writer means learning to pay attention to what you're writing and what you're saying and how you're saying it. Are you making your reader wait to get the main point of your writing because you want her to remain in suspense? Are you slapping the main idea of your writing down on the table? Are you easing into your point? Part of being aware of what you are doing to your reader is being aware of who that reader is.

Who is your reader? Your reader is your personal audience. Every time you write, you write toward a certain group of people, even if you aren't aware of what you're doing. When you write a letter or an email to your mother or father, chances are, it will sound much different from the letter or email you write to your best friend. And the words and phrasing you use with your friends probably differs from the words and phrasing you use with your significant other. Factors such as age, race, and sex can determine how you put your words together, as can your readers' interests, hobbies, professions, and religious and political beliefs.

Consider the television shows that abound (especially with satellite TV). Are most cartoons directed at a group of 30-year-olds, or are they directed at children under 12? What audience do you think the writers of popular shows like <u>Will</u>

and Grace are targeting? What about sports broadcasting? MTV? CNN? BET? Are the features on Animal Planet geared toward people who hate animals? Am I writing this text for John Grisham or Anne Rice? Am I writing this text for graduate students of English? No. I'm writing this for you, freshman composition students. The audience you are writing for determines the way you manipulate your voice—your tone.

You've probably heard someone say, either to you or someone else, "Don't use that tone with me!" Your voice can pack a punch. You can let someone know you're happy, sad, angry, jealous, interested, questioning, confused, overwhelmed, tired, energized (the list goes on and on) all by the tone of your voice. We speak to people differently when we have different objectives. If you're asking permission to do something, the tone of your voice will be much different than if you're confronting a person who has wronged you. Your writing can do the same thing. Especially if you're writing on a subject you feel strongly about, your emotions can seep through your words.

When you write, you need to consider the audience of your work, and you must ask yourself if the tone you are using is appropriate. In other words, don't write with your eyes shut. Make a conscious effort to know what you are writing, to know how that writing comes across, and to know how you WANT that writing to come across. For instance, if you are writing about the horrors that prisoners of war suffer, you probably don't want to use a glib or joking tone. However, if you're writing about the glitzy lives of politicians who speak out for poverty-stricken Americans, that glib tone might work just fine. There are no rights or wrongs, only intentions.

Okay, so you know your audience, you know what you want to say, and you know how you want to say it. Now you need to muster all the self-confidence you have and write with authority. Write as though you've been writing professionally for the last fifty years. Don't be intimidated by degrees. Don't be intimidated by age. Don't be ashamed or embarrassed to express what you feel and what you think. The way you write will determine the way people read your writing.

If you walk into an office building and act as if you know exactly what you are doing and exactly where you are going, people will assume that you do and, in general, they won't question you. Your feeling of power over the words you put on the page is much the same, for if you don't believe in yourself, no one else will believe in you. Write with complete confidence, and your reader will sense it and read your work with trust and respect.

I played the trumpet in high school. My band director always said, "Don't be afraid to belt out your notes. If you're going to be wrong, be WRONG! Play with gusto! There's room for mistakes. There's not room for wimpy attempts." The same thing goes for writing. Don't be hesitant or apologetic about what you put on the page. Those are YOUR WORDS!!! Be proud of them.

3

TB—PREVENTION AND TREATMENT

*I write
because I don't know what I think
until I read what I say.*

—Flannery O'Connor

    Choosing a topic can be one of the hardest things for students in writing courses to do. By *student*, I do not mean writers in the process of learning to write (as writers, we never cease learning). I mean writers who are required, for a class, to choose a topic. There are endless topics worthy of pen and paper or keyboard and screen, but as soon as you are asked to choose one, they all run and hide. They disappear. All a student has to do is think, "I have to come up with a topic," to send those topics to the recesses of the brain, giggling as they hide. There are ways to pull them out of hiding. If you are going to have to choose a topic this semester, lets start digging them out.

    The prophylactic journal. A good way to help prevent TB—"topic block"—is to keep a journal. (And guys, don't worry, *journal* is not politically correct for *diary*.) Your writing will always be stronger if you write from what you know because personal experiences strengthen your papers by adding life and credibility. So many times, we feel that our own lives are boring or that other people will not be interested in our experiences. Just remember, your life is unique. What's old hand to you might be (and often will be) brand new to someone else. A journal helps you remember the things that happen to you and happen around you. It helps you remember those experiences in detail, and it helps you remember how you felt. Flipping through journal entries can bring good topics to the forefront of your mind.

Have you ever had an incredible dream? I had this great dream last night that unfolded like a detective story. But that's all I could tell you now. When I first woke up, I could have related almost every detail of the story. Now, I remember only that the dream was exciting. Things that happen to us on a day-to-day basis are similar. After a while, the details of our experiences fade and we are left with the bare facts of the circumstances.

If you've ever felt your heart break over an ending relationship, felt anger from a fight with your mother or father, or felt elation at an amusement park, you know that after a while you can tell someone, "I broke up with him or her. I had a fight with my parents. I had fun at the fair." But the way your throat felt, the pain in your chest, the sting of tears, the tingling in your finger tips, that feeling of nausea mixed with the sweet smell of cotton candy—those details fade from our memories and become silhouettes of what they once were.

What is journal material? Everything that happens to you. Everyone you meet. Everything you do. Everything you eat. Everything you think about. Everything you dream of. Everything you long for. Everything you despise. Everything. Everything is worthy of your pen and your interpretation.

Some people think they have to write in their journals at night before crawling into bed. Not so. In fact, bedtime is probably one of the worst times to do journal writing. Good journal writing can make it difficult to sleep because it churns up the thoughts in your head. Try writing in the morning as soon as you wake up. Carry a notebook around with you and write as things happen. When you're answering emails, take a few minutes to type up a journal entry (You can make a special file and call it whatever you like. Mine is called Junk.) Write at lunch. Write in the afternoon. Find a good time for you. There is no right or wrong way to do this. And once you make writing a habit, you will find it easier to move your thoughts from your head to the page.

Thirteen Things—an antibiotic. If you don't know what to write about, you don't have a journal to refer to, and you feel all possible topics slowly receding from your grasp into the depths of your mind, you have the first symptoms of "topic block." Don't fret. You may be able to treat your case of TB before it becomes a serious problem and infects each and every creative cell in your brain. Here's what you do.

Stand up. Stretch. Take a few deep breaths while you're still standing. Now sit down and close your eyes. Try to shut everything out of your mind. Take a few more deep breaths. Feel the air enter and exit your lungs. Consciously relax. Now open your eyes and begin writing about one, a few, or all of the following "thirteen things."

THIRTEEN THINGS

1. *things* you believe in

2. *things* you disagree with

3. *things* you used to disagree with that you now agree with

4. *things* you used to believe in but now you don't believe in

5. *things* you have argued about in the past five years (if that list is too long, you can narrow the time (two years, two months, two days)

6. *things* you have felt happy about

7. *things* you have felt sad about

8. *things* you have heard (or overheard) that made you angry

9. *things* you have done that made you feel good about yourself

10. *things* you want from life

10 ½. *things* that need to change.

11. *things* you are afraid of

12. *things* you have learned about yourself in the last three years

13. *things* you have learned about people in general

After you have made your lists, try to answer one or all of the 5Ws and big H (Who, What, When, Where, Why, How) for each. Remember there's no right or wrong way to answer these, so be creative. If you believe in animal rights, you can ask yourself, Who deserves animal rights. What needs to be done to help the animal rights cause? When should animals have rights? Where do animals have no rights? Why should animals have rights? How (in what way or manner) should laws change to include animal rights?

Okay. Now, out of the mess of words and phrases you have written, circle the ones that, for whatever reason, appeal to you the most. Pull out a fresh sheet of paper or open a new document on the computer. Write the words or phrases you circled at the top. Now, with those words in mind, start writing.

Write anything and everything that comes into your head. Don't stop to think. Don't stop writing. Allow yourself to go off on tangents. Follow the movements of your mind. Be a slave to your thoughts. Don't try to control what comes out. Don't be a dictator. Simply record the flow. If you have a timer, set it between five and ten minutes. This process, the idea of which first came from Peter Elbow, is known as freewriting.

Now stand up again and stretch. Take a few deep breaths. Walk around if you want, but don't go too far. Sit back down. Take another deep breath, and read what you have written. Once again, circle the phrases and words that call out to you.

If necessary, do the entire process again, and again, and again. Eventually, your mind will show you what you need to write about.

Extreme Measures. If you have a hard time coming up with answers to the above questions, you may have a full-blown infection of "topic block." To overcome such a bout of TB, you need to forget about your paper, forget about writing, and stop worrying. You must relax. Go do something you enjoy. Step outside and enjoy the sun or rain or heat or cold. Go to the gym. Ride a bike. See a movie. Make a batch of cookies. Play with your pets. Go for a run or a walk. Go fishing. Go to the beach. Change the wallpaper. Put on a CD and dance. Take a shower. Fold your clothes. Make your bed. DO SOMETHING ACTIVE. Playing video games or flipping through the channels on the television doesn't help. Shift your attention. Change your scenery. Get out of the house, if necessary. Do what you need to do to clear your head.

If you continue to freeze up, even after you have switched gears and taken your mind off the assignment, try talking to a friend. Be positive in your conversation. Don't spend an hour complaining that you can't think of anything to write about. Spend that hour forcing yourself to work through ideas out loud, probing your friend for advice and suggestions.

Remember, the topic you choose does not have to be "life-shattering." You don't have to solve the problem of world hunger. You don't have to predict the next world war. You don't even have to deal with the ethical issues of space exploration. Ambition is great. I don't want to hold you back. But keep in mind that some of the most radical and world-changing ideas started small. Rosa Parks didn't take on every aspect of racism; she just didn't want to give up her seat on the bus. Now look how far we've come.

4

THE STRAIGHT AND NARROW

*A writer is a person for whom writing
is more difficult than it is for other people.*

—*Thomas Mann*

Once you have a topic to write about, you must make sure it is the right size. If your topic is too broad (the case for most comp students), you will have a difficult time organizing your thoughts. If your topic is too small, you won't be able to write enough. Either way your paper will be harder to write than it needs to be. You want to be like Goldilocks and find a middle ground that's "just right" so you don't spend unnecessary hours struggling with what you want to say.

Learning to narrow a topic can be difficult. Generally, if you feel your topic is too specific to write about, you probably have a perfect topic. The papers you will write in many of your university classes (especially during your first two years) will be only 4–8 pages in length, so you want a topic narrow enough for you to handle in 4–8 pages, not a topic that would require 50 pages to deal with effectively. What's the difference? Consider the following:

Parking in the United States is a growing problem.

This is a book. You would have to consider each separate state and the cities that make up those states. You can narrow this idea by focusing on one state.

Parking in Florida is a growing problem.

This is still book-length. You would have to consider too many cities and those cities' individual problems with parking. You can narrow this idea by focusing on one city. Also, you need a time frame. Has parking in Florida always been a problem? Well, no. There was a time when we didn't have cars.

Parking in Pensacola has become a growing problem during the last five years.

Now we're getting there, but this is still too much for a 4–6-page paper. You can narrow this idea by choosing a specific location where parking is a problem, or by focusing on certain individuals who have problems with parking (people with disabilities, for instance).

Parking at Gulf Breeze High School has become a serious problem for students during the last five years.

Now we're talking! The focus of this paper points to one place, to one group of people, and to one specific period. This topic would be much easier to work with than the first.

Angie, a former student, wrote her first paper on discrimination against women. She wrote a wonderful paragraph on each of the following ideas: gender stereotyping of young children, double standards for men and women, pay discrepancies between men and women in the workplace, and prohibition of women in combat. Each of those paragraphs, however, could have been a paper in itself and deserved more than a paragraph of thought.

When you feel you've narrowed your ideas to something you can work with, you have to develop those ideas by discovering the materials you will need to express yourself. What are the materials? Details. Examples. Facts. Figures. Anecdotes. Comparisons. Contrasts. Descriptions. Quotations. Analogies. Anything that will help you communicate what you want to say about your topic is material. Your paper is a sculpture. Once you have an idea about what you would like to sculpt, you have to find your clay.

5

THE CLAY

*The discipline of the writer is to learn to be still
and listen to what his subject has to tell him.*

—Rachel Carson

Finding your clay, what composition instructors often call prewriting, means probing your mind for material you can work with. Trying to leap from the conception of an idea to a complete paper is like trying to make it across a stream without stepping on a few stones or getting your feet wet—it's close to impossible. You need to explore your topic before trying to organize your ideas into a paper. The following techniques can help you move from your original idea through writing your first draft.

Brainstorming. Think about your topic and jot down all the words that come to mind. Keep listing until you cannot think of anything else that relates to your topic. Then look over your list. Some people like to use this list to help organize their thoughts on a subject before they begin writing. Many times, once the words are out of your head and down on paper (or screen), it's easier for you to work with them.

You can brainstorm with each word from your first list, forming subordinate lists, to help draw everything out of your mind. You can continue to brainstorm with each word of each subordinate list until you find it impossible to go further. When you look over your *topic inventory*, you can cross out random words that don't apply to your topic.

Sometimes mischievous words slip in, trying to throw you off. You have to play search and destroy with those guys because they can lead you off track. Other times, though, what at first seems like a word trying to weasel its way into your paper is really the clever paths of your mind showing you important connections that you might have otherwise overlooked. You simply have to use good judgment.

Building a Web. Also called Mapping or Branching, Building a Web is the first cousin of Brainstorming. The process is the same. Only the method differs. You begin by writing down your topic and circling it. You then think of ideas (words or phrases) that come to your mind when you think of your topic. You write down those ideas in the area around your topic, circling each subordinate idea and connecting them to your main topic with a line. You continue to do this with each new circle, adding details, facts, and examples that relate to your ideas.

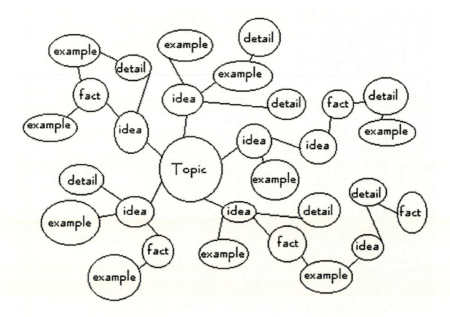

There's no right or wrong way to draw this out. You can follow one line of thinking until you cannot think of anything else, and then go back to the first circle. Or you can systematically list all the words that come to you in circles around each word. I call this b*uilding a web*, rather than mapping or branching, because by connecting each idea, your thoughts form a web that will trap your ideas in a pattern so that you can come back to them and see how they work together.

Freewriting. You worked with freewriting to find a topic. You can also use freewriting to explore your topic. You can do this before, instead of, or after brainstorming or building a web. Whether you are composing on the screen (which I prefer) or whether you are using pen and paper (as I'm actually doing right now), the blank screen/page can be terribly intimidating. Even if we have an idea swirling in our heads, it is often difficult to write that first sentence. And so many times, that first sentence comes out sounding ridiculous.

My answer to this fear? Write. Write. Write. Write anything. Write everything. Write nonsense. Write until what you want to say comes out. Write until the very act of writing drags your thoughts into words. Don't be afraid of not making sense or not being "good." Don't fuss with grammar. Don't worry about introductions, organization, or spelling. Don't even read over what you're writing until you've emptied your mind of all thoughts. Just write. Write everything that flows from your mind, even if it seems off your topic.

Sometimes it's a good idea to make yourself write for a specified time, say twenty minutes. Use a timer if you have one. Don't stop to think things out. If you come to bump in the road where your mind refuses to feed your hands anything to put on the page, don't stop writing. Instead, write "I'm writing, I'm writing, I'm writing, I'm writing" or continue re-writing the last word you wrote until your mind gives up and starts feeding you fresh words again.

Controlled freewriting can help you write the first draft of your paper once you have found and explored a good topic. Read over your topic, your web, your brainstorming lists, and/or your freewriting. Review your first freewriting exercises if you used them to find a topic. Start writing. Once again, don't worry about introductions, organization, grammar, or spelling. If you have a certain introduction in mind, feel free to write it, but don't worry if you don't. You can write one later.

Don't worry about the way your writing sounds. Just write.

When you come to a bumpy place, go back and read what you've written. Stop and think about the things you want to say. You don't have to do this at one setting. You can write for a while, go do other things, come back to writing, get some sleep, come back to writing, make some phone calls, come back to writing, etc. Each time you return to your writing, or each time you feel you've exhausted one line of thought, review your topic, your web, your freewriting, and/or your brainstorming lists again.

Don't worry about how your ideas fit together. Don't worry if you repeat yourself. You want to get stuff on the page so you have raw material to work with. Write until you feel there is simply nothing more to write about. Then write a little more. Now you have your clay. You're finally ready to begin sculpting.

6

LISTENING TO THE PAGE

*Every story finds its own form. Finding that form
is the great struggle of writing, for which there is no prescription.*

—Garrison Keillor

    The first part of sculpting is discovering the main idea of what you have written. You may be thinking, "Wait a minute! I already have a main idea!" Sometimes, even when we start with a good, focused idea, and even when we spend time creating material to work with by brainstorming, webbing, and freewriting, our ideas shift while we're writing. Such shifts are normal and often reveal the true point of what we want to say, so don't worry if you find your ideas have changed. How do you discover the main idea of your writing?

    Print out a copy of your controlled freewriting. Read through what you've written from start to finish without doing anything. Read out loud. After you've read it once, find a pen or pencil, and read it again. Circle the sections that focus on the same ideas and label them. You may have two or three (or more) sections of your writing that focus on the same specific ideas but that are not spatially connected.

    Go back to the computer and cut and paste, placing similar ideas in the same sections. Make paragraphs out of those sections by indenting the beginning of the first line five spaces (one tab). Don't worry about how those sentences work together right now. Just make sure that you've separated individual ideas into individual paragraphs.

    Once you have created your paragraphs, read the paper again to insure that you have sent your subjects to their proper homes. If you want, you can combine or delete repetitive sentences, but it's not necessary at this point. Print out a new copy. Now you're beginning to shape your clay.

At this stage, it's a good idea to set your writing aside and do something else. Read something for another class. Get some air. Go to bed. Eat a snack. Watch a little TV. Just get away from the paper.

When you're ready to get back to the paper, settle into a chair (or whatever comfortable place you like to work), and read the last printout of your writing. What is your paper saying? Forget about the ideas you started with. Erase them from your mind. The only things that exist now are the words on the pages you hold. Allow me to repeat: the only things that exist now are the words on the pages you hold. Read those words closely. Read them two or three times if necessary. Then pull out a scratch sheet of paper and write down the main idea of your paper.

Now look over your initial notes, your first ideas. Has your topic changed? If your ideas have changed significantly or shifted in meaning, you should brainstorm, build a web, or freewrite with your new topic to flesh it out; then add to your controlled freewriting using the new material you come up with. Go through these preliminary steps of organization again until you feel comfortable with the amount of material you have. Read what you've written, and write down the main idea of your paper again and compare it to your lists.

In the study of composition, this main idea is called the thesis statement. I have found that many students (too many students) still cower at the very word *thesis*. It's like mentioning a special type of torture. Well, ease your fears. The idea of a thesis should not intimidate you. Contrary to what you might have been told, there's not one right way to write a thesis. In fact, for right now, I don't want you to worry about trying to write a thesis at all. The thesis will come.

There's an 80's movie called *Field of Dreams*. The main character (Kevin Costner) hears voices that tell him, "If you build it, they will come." (He builds a baseball field in his cornfield and famous ball players who have died come to play baseball). Well, your thesis statement is just like those dead ball players. "If you write, it will come."

Write the paper. Let your ideas out. I promise you, your thesis will appear. And you will quickly learn that having a thesis is not as difficult or scary as it may seem. In fact, let's ditch the word <u>thesis</u>. Why don't we use <u>point</u> instead? You've heard people ask, "So, what's the point?" What they're asking for is a thesis, plain and simple.

Depending on what you are writing and depending on how you want your work to read and depending on what you want your paper to do, your point can and will take many different forms. You may want to reveal the point of your piece bit by bit; you may want to make a forceful statement in the very beginning which declares your point; or you may even want to wait until the end of what you are writing to reveal your purpose, your point. Sometimes the writing itself, taken as a whole, whispers the point to the reader. It just depends on what you want to do. However, beginning writers beware. If your readers do not have a sense, right away, of what you are trying to say, they will stop reading. Putting your thesis, your point, near the beginning of your paper or at the end of the first paragraph, is usually the best course of action.

Organization. Once you've determined what your paper is saying, you must insure that stray ideas or thoughts do not hinder its message. You're ready to plunge into the big O—organization. The big O is one of the most important parts of a paper. Your skill at organizing your thoughts can make your paper strong or destroy it from the beginning.

Consider your paper as your part in a conversation. Generally, when we talk to people, especially if we talk to them about something we feel strongly about, we keep our ideas together. If we mention the reasons we enjoy the beach and the sun, we don't throw in a comment about goofy golf. Now, I'm sure there are those of you who are remembering playing goofy golf at a place on the beach and saying "I would talk about goofy golf if I were talking about the beach." Great. The point is this: you want to keep your ideas focused, and you want your ideas to flow smoothly.

Think of dominoes. If you line up a group of dominoes and tip over the first in line, each one will touch the other and they will all fall in a sequence. If you're really good at setting up patterns, you can make spirals and use bridges and make two or three different lines come off of one line and then fit back together. But if some of the dominoes are too far apart or you don't position them in direct line with one other, the momentum will stop.

Writing is the same way. You want to line up your thoughts so tightly that your reader has no choice but to *fall*-ow through. If you have awkward places in your writing or thoughts that don't connect well, your reader may lose sight of your point, just like the dominoes coming to an abrupt halt.

So how do you organize a paper? Well, if you've done your controlled free-writing and you've gone through the process of circling and labeling similar ideas, you have already begun.

The paragraph is your tool for organization. With the paragraph, you do three things at the same time: you keep your reader's attention, you divide ideas, and you clear the reader's path. Excessively long paragraphs can make your reader's attention falter because any large block of information with no separation acts as a sleeping pill.

Paragraphs let your reader breathe. Pretend that you have to hold your breath while you read. The five spaces at the beginning of each new paragraph give you permission to take a breath, but you can breathe only between paragraphs. You can use this method to gauge the length of your own paragraphs, as long as you realize that such a measurement of length will not work in every case.

Paragraphs can be as short as you need them to be.

Now that you have separated your ideas, you must deal with each paragraph individually. Read the paragraph out loud so you can get a feel for what you are saying. Read slowly. Don't rush. Combine sentences that say the same thing in different ways. Remove any sentences that don't belong. If you don't want to delete those stray sentences for good, you can cut them and paste them in a new document.

Read the paragraph aloud once again. Begin to pay attention to how your sentences sound. How do they work together? Play with their placement in the paragraph. Move them around. Add to the ideas of your paragraph. Enhance what you have written. Whenever you make a few changes, read the paragraph aloud again. Do this with every paragraph you have. Don't let yourself feel intimidated by the words on the page. Those are YOUR WORDS. Only you can command them.

Once you've worked through each of your paragraphs, read your paper from beginning to end. Are your paragraphs arranged the way you want? Can you follow the progression of your ideas from paragraph to paragraph? Play with the structure of your paper. Don't be afraid to toy with different ways of laying out your thoughts.

Continue to read the paper out loud after every change. Now you can check for detail and support. Do you provide examples, personal experiences, and/or quotations from outside sources to support your statements? Are there places in your paper that might improve with additional details or explanations?

Transitions. This is another one of those intimidating words. Why? Probably because there are a number of students (English majors included) who sail through college never knowing for certain what a good transition sentence or transition paragraph looks like. What is a transition? Forget about writing for a minute. A transition is moving from one place or situation to another. It's about movement. It's about change.

Learning to ride a Honda 500 Silverwing is a good transition from riding a Honda 250 Reflex to riding a Harley 1200 Sportster. Instead of moving from barely any power (the 250) to a bike that might leave you behind on the pavement (the 1200) without anything in between, you move up a notch to the 500, which won't quite leave you behind, but will teach you how to control a heavier, more powerful bike.

You can make a similar analogy with almost anything. Transitions help us move from one situation to another without being left sitting on the pavement, wondering what happened. You want to take your reader through your writing without making him feel jarred or jerked around.

You want your reader to feel as if he's cruising down a river in a canoe. Your words are the current. You don't want him to have get out of the water and pull the canoe up on land to maneuver around logs that prevent him from continuing down the river. You don't want him to struggle that much. Your ideas should blend so well that when you switch from one paragraph to the next, or from one sentence to the next, your reader doesn't even notice the ripples in the current.

My advice: don't worry about how to write a good transition. Don't even think about *transitions*. Worry about the flow of your writing. When you feel there is an abrupt change of ideas in your work (the dominoes come to a halt), simply look for a way to ease your reader from point A to point B. The best way to write a good transition is to not realize that you've written a transition at all. According to Peter Elbow, "If you have to make introductions or transitions, you have things in the wrong order. If they were in the right order they wouldn't need introductions or transitions" (41).

By taking you through the above steps, I've given you a process for writing a paper. These are not the ONLY steps you can use. This is not the ONLY process that produces good papers. I've given you what I believe works best, especially for beginning writers. You can use this process for any type of paper or story you write.

All I can give you, however, is the process. I can't tell you exactly what a thesis—a point—should look like. I can't tell you exactly how you should organize your paper. I can't tell you exactly how to do anything because the fine points of writing, of good writing, can never be categorized. Something mystical happens during the writing process that I cannot relate to you in words. Something special occurs. Perhaps that something is called inspiration. Perhaps it's our subconscious opening the doors to all those hidden pathways of the mind. You must experience it for yourself. And you WILL experience it if you allow yourself to give in to your writing, listen to the page, and work with what you've written.

7

SAYING HELLO

*I always write a good first line,
but I have trouble in writing the others.*

—Molière

If you want someone to read your work of his or her own accord, you have to introduce your writing in a way that will grab your reader's attention. Sometimes the introductions to your papers will come easily, writing themselves in without your being aware of it. Other times, however, you may have no idea how to lead your reader into your paper.

This chapter will provide you with a few tried and true methods to introduce a piece of writing along with examples from student papers to show you how those methods work.

Tell a story. You can use a personal experience or an anecdote (a brief account of an event) to pull your reader into the paper. Often, this approach is both fun to write and fun to read.

Three weeks ago on a Wednesday night, my roommate and I were busting our butts studying for a test in Calculus II.. At 2:00 AM, I mentioned the idea of doughnuts. By 4:00 AM, the thought of hot doughnuts melting in our mouths had settled in our brains. We both began the hunt for sufficient funds to satisfy our need. He gathered all of the change on his desk, while I searched through the pockets of my coats. Between the two of us, we had $2.18. We finally made the 20-minute drive downtown to see the bright, flashing "Hot Donuts" sign.

I could practically taste the grape jelly soothing my mouth, putting my mind at rest in doughnut euphoria. We walked in and could smell the precious, ever so sweet doughnuts that were waiting for us. We were appalled, however, to find that a dozen glazed doughnuts cost $3.49. I promptly asked for a student discount. They didn't have one. A single jelly doughnut was $.69. We had to split 5 glazed doughnuts, and *my dreams of eating doughnuts until I made myself sick slipped out the window.*—Jibri Nuriddin (a paper about the need for student discounts in Pensacola, Florida.)

Use a quotation. A good quotation can encompass the entire theme of your writing in someone else's words. Depending on whom you quote, quotations can add credibility to your work.

"The inmate died at ten thirty…the suicide on April 13 was the third at the high-maximum security facility since it opened in 1998. All three men died by hanging, their bed sheets fashioned into nooses."
—Nathan Blanchfield (a paper about the similarities between the new high technology, maximum-security prisons and solitary confinement)

Define an unfamiliar term. Beginning with a definition plays on the curiosity of your readers. This method works best if the word is unusual or the definition sparks interest.

<u>Spam</u>, "internet junk mail such as solicitations for chain letters, pyramid schemes, get-rich-quick instruction methods, and invitations to buy pornography," is becoming an increasing problem for Internet users.
—Marianna Bosnjakovic (a paper explaining options available for people who hate unsolicited internet junk mail)

Directly state your argument. Especially if your topic is controversial, a forceful statement can draw the attention of readers with opposing viewpoints as well as readers who share your opinion.

The State of Florida should allow gay and lesbian couples to adopt children.
—Chelle Staton (a paper about homosexual rights to adoption)

Write in the reader. If you want your reader to experience some aspect that you want to convey, you can write them into your paper by using <u>you</u>.

You are jammed into a crowded room like sardines in a can. The temperature feels like zero degrees and falling. You sit down at a desk surrounded by other anxious bodies, waiting for what is to come next. The speaker slowly reads you the directions. Assistants hand out the booklets and the #2 pencils. Finally you hear, "You may begin with section one of the test."

You open your test booklet and begin pondering over the questions inside. You find yourself dwelling over one question for what seems like forever. You begin to wonder what the question is even asking you, and you notice the air conditioner has begun to make a slight humming noise. You haven't finished the section, but you hear a crackly voice say, "Stop. Please close your test booklets. You have now completed section one of the test." Your body tenses as you picture you life going down hill fast.
—Angie Cooke (a paper about the evils of standardized testing)

Be Creative. When all else fails—be creative.
I have thoughts in my brain that travel a thousand miles per hour,
so dirty down south I might need to take a shower.
So many lives lost over the money and the power
Its outrageous. Its contagious.
Like a habit or a common cold, whether young or old, in the game or fold,
I know I can't be another victim in the streets, another casualty.
So before my life ends I keep my mind over matter
and won't stop fighting until I reach the top of the ladder.
—Mike Shea (a paper defending the positive aspects of rap music, with the intro in rap lyrics)

There is no right or wrong way to introduce a paper. Your goal is to catch your reader's attention and make her want to read the paper. You won't know if something works until you try it, so have fun. Play with the different methods of introduction I have shown you in this chapter, and don't hesitate to invent your own.

8

A NOTE ON THE FRIDGE

*Life is the art of drawing sufficient conclusions
from insufficient premises.*

—Samuel Butler

When you discover a topic you want to write about, you can usually find the words to get your point across. And more often than not, with a little creativity and thought, you can think of a good introduction to draw your readers in and grab their attention. But once you have your ideas down on paper and an intro you're happy with, how in the world do you write a conclusion? What is a conclusion anyway? And what's it supposed to do for your reader?

I've heard many instructors tell students, "The concluding paragraph is the last chance you have to convince a reader of your point." I believe such a statement is misleading. Really, if you have not convinced your reader to see your side by the time you reach your conclusion, you're NOT going to convince him. When students view their conclusion as "last chance" to make their point, they inevitably kill the concluding paragraph by doing one (or more) of three things you should never do to end a paper.

*NEVER restate the main idea of a paper in different words. The attempt is predictable, boring, and ineffective. You don't want to be repetitious in the heart of your paper, so why would you want the last thing you leave your reader with to sound repetitive?

*NEVER introduce new questions or bring up new subjects. Bringing up new ideas leaves your reader feeling that your paper is incomplete. If you're going to discuss a new idea, discuss it in the paper, not in the conclusion.

*NEVER undermine your own writing by apologizing for not being an expert or saying, "this is only my opinion." When you write, write with authority. Be confident. Be the expert. Your attitude shows through your writing.

So, if a conclusion is not a "last chance" for persuasion, what is it? Your introduction grabs your reader's attention. The heart of your paper provides the reader with evidence to support your claims. A conclusion should leave your reader with something to make your essay memorable, something to keep your ideas alive in your reader's head long after he has ceased reading. The following methods are good ways to do just that.

Come Full Circle: A common, but effective, type of conclusion relates back to the beginning of the paper. This does NOT mean repeating what you have already said in different words. This means finding a way to make your reader feel he has come full circle. You can use something from your introduction or you can use the title of your work to create this circular conclusion. I gave chapter eight the title "The Pink Tummy of Writing" because I wanted to give my reader the image of a pink, vulnerable puppy tummy, and make him wonder, "What in the world does a pink tummy have to do with writing?" I conclude chapter eight by saying,

> *"To improve, we have to be willing to bare the vulnerable pink tummy of our writing. So roll over, and let the criticism begin."*

By itself, those sentences probably do the job. But connected to the title, I think they give a better sense that I have "wrapped things up."

Predict an Outcome: You can make a prediction based on the evidence you have presented. Alec Blome's paper on Gambling in Pensacola ends with this type of conclusion.

> *"When casinos are finally legalized in Pensacola, Florida, our community will flourish."*

Draw a Conclusion: You can draw conclusions from evidence presented in your paper without restating your argument. Scientific writing based on the results of experiments relies on this technique.

> Though sucralose is thought to be a good substitute for sugar, the fact that it reacts with yeast the same way regular sugar does suggests that our body will metabolizes both sucralose and sugar in the same way, creating negligible differences in the affect on blood-sugar levels. Sucralose, then, is not a proper substitute for glucose, and should not be used as a weight-loss product.

Use a Quotation: The same way you can begin a paper with a quotation to lend authority to your writing and encompass the message of your paper, you can end a paper with a quotation. Sometimes our words are not enough, and leaving the reader with the connection between what you have written and quote from a familiar, reliable source can have a lasting impact. The following conclusion is taken from "How Did Hemingway Write?" by Allen Josephs:

> *Naturally I have saved the best for last; here is Hemingway's ultimate secret. George Plimpton asks Hemingway in the Paris Review how much rewriting he does:*
> *Hemingway: It depends. I re-wrote the ending to A Farewell to Arms, the last page of it, 39 times before I was satisfied.*
> *Plimpton: Was there some technical problem there? What was it that stumped you?*
> *Hemingway: Getting the words right.*

Make an Analogy: You can use analogies to leave your reader with a lasting impression and enforce your point by making a connection. You know by now how fond I am of analogies, and I am particularly fond of my conclusion for chapter three. I tell you that you do not have to take on the world with your topic, and I conclude by stating,

> "Rosa Parks didn't take on every aspect of racism; she simply wanted to sit in the front of the bus. Now look how far we've come."

Clearly, discovering a topic and racism are completely different ideas. But I wanted to leave you with the notion that what might seem "small potatoes" to you could be more powerful than something that seems outwardly dramatic. I also wanted to leave you with a good feeling, and I wanted to inspire you. Just thinking about the guts it took for Rosa Parks to sit in the front of that bus does both for me. I took the chance, hoping it would do the same for you.

Give a Command: You can end your writing with a firm statement that encourages your reader to take action. Katerina Pugh used this type of forceful conclusion to end her paper, titled "Limbo Learning," about the problems students who speak English as a second language encounter when they do not fit into the American student category, but are not considered international students.

> "The university should take a look at the two-category system and recognize that there are students who are not represented, students who fall through the cracks."

You can also use this type of conclusion to leave your reader with a certain feeling instead of a specific call for action. I try to constantly instill in you the idea that YOU are in charge of your life and your writing. I conclude my introduction by saying, "Above all, have faith in yourself." And I conclude chapter three by saying, "Don't be hesitant or apologetic about what you put on the page. Those are YOUR WORDS!! Be proud of them."

Acknowledge Doubt: If the point of your writing is to provoke thought on a religious issue (such as reincarnation) or an "unsolvable" question (such as life on other planets), you can conclude your paper by stating that your purpose was not to make a dogmatic claim, nor to "discover" an answer, but to suggest possibilities. Your willingness to acknowledge controversy and mystery can make your writing stronger. Be careful, however, that you do not use this approach to avoid doing research or giving adequate thought to a subject. Also, avoid answering your own questions with "I don't know." If you knew, you would have told your reader by this time. A better answer in this particular style is "I hope not." Or "I like to think so."

> Is there life on other planets? I like to think so. But whether we are alone in the universe or one of millions of species, the way we treat one other and the way we treat other cultures will determine how future generations see us. And if we're not alone, perhaps our struggle for peace can and will be a testament to our love and respect for life and a means to connect with those people who exist "where no one has gone before."

Spring your Point: If you have waited to declare the point of your writing until the end of your paper, you can conclude your writing by pointing out the significance of the evidence you have presented. If your point is extremely controversial, waiting until the end to spring your purpose on your reader can be effective, especially if you are holding his attention and gaining his support and making him think the writing is actually going in another direction. Such writing can cause a reader to rethink his position on a subject, especially if he is unaware of where you are taking him. To make this technique work, however, you must give your reader some reason to continue waiting for you to make your point clear. This is probably the most difficult type of writing to pull off because you risk loosing your reader at any minute if he doesn't know where you are going. So again, new writers beware. The following is the conclusion to a paper which seemed to be about cruel animal testing procedures.

> *So, you buy make-up and lotions not tested on animals. Good. But have you given much thought to which eggs you purchase? Millions of hens are placed in cages so small they cannot move. Their legs never touch the ground, so they lose the ability to walk. They never know what the sky looks like, only the fluorescent lights as they sit in their own feces waiting for a harsh spray of water to wash them down or a machine to take their eggs away. These hens suffer as much as animals subjected to inhumane testing procedures. So next time you're at the grocery store, look for eggs that specify—free range hens. Only then can you be sure you're not participating in the meaningless torture of animals for convenience.*

Leave well enough alone: Sometimes, our writing can stand on its own without what we think of as a conclusion. If you have a number of points to argue, you can try leaving the most powerful one for last, and end there. Sometimes, with powerful arguments, going back to "recap" can kill the momentum and emotion of the paper. Unless this particular technique is executed properly, however, the reader will feel that you've left him hanging or that he's missing a page.

The above methods of conclusion can give your papers powerful endings, but keep those endings brief. If you have ever walked "family" to the door after an extended vacation when everyone is tired and has had TOO much of each other's company, you know that long goodbyes can be excruciating. Your paper is a visit with your reader, and he will know when your writing is coming to a close. So don't let your conclusion overstay its welcome. Sometimes it's better just to leave a note on the fridge and walk away. Your visit will speak for itself.

9

STAGES OF REVISION

I have the words already. What I am seeking is the perfect order of words in the sentence. You can see for yourself how many different ways they might be arranged.

—*James Joyce*

Oh no! Dreaded revision. If you have put hard work into organizing your paper and making your ideas flow, you probably feel as if you have already revised your work. You have. No real separation exists between writing and revising. Revision isn't something you do AFTER you write. Revision is an ongoing process of upheaval and change. Writing IS revising. And all writing (I have yet to learn of an exception) can bear improvement. There are three different stages of revision. You have probably already experienced the first.

The First Stage: Transforming Your Thoughts Into Words

Chapters 5 and 6 take you through the first stage of revision. You have to decide what you want to say, SO YOU WRITE; then you decide if you've said it. You have to include details and support, SO YOU WRITE; then you check to see if you've included enough or too much. You have to organize your words, SO YOU WRITE; then you go back to see if the arrangement of ideas pleases you. You want your ideas to flow smoothly, SO YOU WRITE; then you read through and see if they do.

This first stage of revision could include, technically, twenty or more drafts. In this age of computers, however, drafts aren't always tangible. Your writing might go through several changes while still on the screen. I want you to try to get away from thinking about "drafts." Too many students rely on the number of drafts they have completed to gauge the perfection of their papers. Writing doesn't work that way. While the amount of time you spend working on your paper is probably proportionate to the success of that paper, no certain number of drafts can insure good writing.

The second stage: Playing the Reader
You've worked hard to write your paper, and you like what you've written. You've organized your thoughts. Your thoughts flow. You've included details and support, anecdotes and definitions. You've read through what you've written more times than you want to count or admit. You feel you paper is finished. Good. It's time for you to move into the second stage of revision. Unfortunately, many students think they have a "final draft" when they haven't even finished the first stage of revision. I've told you that writing isn't easy. It's not a speedy process either.

The second stage of revision relies on a good first stage and SPACE. You have to give your paper room to breathe. Only by getting away from your work can you see your ideas in a new light. When you do, you will often discover things you would have otherwise overlooked. Ideally, you should set your work aside for at least a week. Most students don't have adequate time to spend away from their drafts. If you can't let your paper rest for a week, at least try to leave it untouched overnight.

When you return to your writing, pretend you are reading it for the first time. Don't do this reading on the screen. Use a printed copy so you can make marks and so you can see how your words look on the page. You must try to separate yourself from what you think is already in the paper in order to discover what the paper needs. To do this, you must learn to approach your writing from the reader's perspective.

Donald Murray, a professional writer for more than sixty years and a renowned teacher of writing, tells us in his textbook The Craft of Revision that "any piece of writing is a conversation with a reader who interrupts to say: How Come? How do you know that? Says who? I don't get it? What do you mean? I'd like to know more about that. No Kidding. Why'd she do that? What'd he do then? Tell me more. Stop it. Enough already. Get to the point. Whoa. Back up. I don't understand. Whatta you mean 'gaseous diffusion'?"

If your reader can say any of these things while reading your work, you have not done enough to express your ideas. As a result, he or she may begin to feel lost, distrustful, and/or confused—and more often than not, stop reading. You have to learn what to cut, what to change, and what to add to help your reader understand the material you are trying to relate.

What to Cut:
Writers, both new and old, often have weak stomachs when it comes to cutting. Revision can be difficult, bloody work. Those are your words, your babies,

on the page, and if you've worked long and hard to pull your thoughts out and trap them on paper, the idea of cutting can be painful. Nine times out of ten, however, that cutting is necessary to clarify your points and make your paper easier to read.

Students usually have a hard time cutting material because they have been forced to write papers of specified length. Kate Ronald, professor of English at Miami University, writes, "I know [cutting] isn't easy, especially in school, where you've been trained to 'write 1000 words' and, by God, you'll write 1000 words whether you have one or 1000 words to say on the subject. Try to stop padding and counting words in the margins. Cut words. This is probably the most practical piece of advice I have" (180). Long papers are not inherently better than shorter papers. Who can say that eight pages are better than four if he doesn't know the subject? The length of your paper depends on what you want to say, so only you can decide what length it needs to be.

It is common for writers to repeat themselves. That's how the brain works when it's trying to word ideas in an intelligible form. We gather those ideas by writing, but we have to re-order those ideas to make our writing better. Many times, you can combine two sentences (sometimes three, four, or five) that say the same thing to form a stronger sentence.

Wordiness is the enemy of all good writing. You don't want your ideas to get tangled in your words. Using excessive connector words such as *to* and *that* can weaken your message, as can beginning sentences with *it is*, *there are*, or *there is*, using two or more adjectives that mean the same thing, or using an adjective when the noun it modifies already implies the adjective's meaning. Consider the following:

Wordy: The car that I like is the one that has the turbo engine that is unlike any other car that is made today.
Improved: I like the car with the unique turbo engine.

Wordy: It is true that all freshmen at UWF must take composition I.
Improved: All freshmen at UWF must take composition I.

Wordy: There are no other lanes open.
Improved: No other lanes are open.

Wordy: The curious, inquisitive cat sat by the door of the large mansion.
Improved: The curious cat sat by the door of the mansion (<u>mansion</u> implies <u>large</u>, <u>curious</u> implies <u>inquisitive</u>).

Writing that leads the reader away from your main point without a specific reason can be dangerous. Your paper will seem disorganized, and your reader will become confused. Even if you only suspect that a sentence might be pushing the limits of your paper, cut it out. You can always paste it back in later. When you eradicate the random paths of your ideas and concentrate on your point, your paper will develop power.

Sometimes writers try to disguise the problems in their papers with excessive description. You can give a magnificent paint job to a broken-down car, but it's still going to be a broken-down car. You want to put your reader into your writing and help him see what you see, not make him wade through meaningless, flowery details. Writing with too much description can bore the reader. There's a fine line between giving too little and giving too much. You have to walk it with care.

"Murdering your darlings" is probably the hardest part of cutting. When you write, you will inevitably form phrases, use words, tell stories, or structure sentences in ways that make you smile. You'll fall in love with an image or a certain word. You will catch yourself grinning as you read something special you've written. Unfortunately, those are sometimes the very parts that need to be taken out. And they're the hardest to let go of. The easiest thing to do is grit your teeth, cut the part, and read your work without it. As I've said before, you can always put it back. You may find that when the child of your creation is gone, your writing becomes stronger.

What to Avoid:

Clichés. You never want your writing to be ordinary or predictable, so don't use clichés. What's a cliché? If you can hear or read the first part of a phrase and know exactly what is to follow, you've found one. Fill in the blanks of the following sentences to see what I mean.

Every cloud has _____. I need this like I need _____.
He's as blind as a _____.
Things must get worse before they _____.
Last but not _____. I feel as sick as a _____.

Clichés are common in our daily speech, so when you freewrite, they appear. That's okay. That doesn't say anything bad about you as a writer. You just need to recognize clichés so you can change your wording to something more original.

Passive sentence constructions are thieves. They weaken your writing by stealing action. In an active sentence, the subject acts on the predicate. In a passive sentence, the subject is acted upon by the predicate. The passive is NOT simply using the verbs *am, is, are, was, and were*. A passive sentence includes these verbs as helping verbs, but also explains "who" or "what" is doing the action with *by*.

Passive: I was stopped **by the policeman**.
Active: The policeman stopped me. (active verb = stopped)
Sometimes the "by" phrase does not appear in the sentence, but the sentence remains passive because you can add the "by" phrase to the end.
Passive: Jason is loved. (He has to be loved BY somebody)
Active: Everyone loves Jason. (active verb = loves)
Is using the passive always wrong? No. But the more you use active verbs, the more active your writing will sound.

Monotony. If you use the same words again and again and again and again, your writing will become predictable and tedious. English has a variety of words at your disposal. Use them. Teachers sometimes tell students not to use a thesaurus. For me, that's like telling a student not to use a dictionary. Even if you're just searching for a way to explain something, using a thesaurus can help trigger the thoughts in your head by giving you an interesting word to play with.

Before you choose a fresh word from the pages of a thesaurus, however, make sure to look that word up in a good dictionary. Not all words listed under the same heading will have the same connotations or even the same meanings. So, be careful. For instance, under *honor* in *Roget's Thesaurus* is *ornament*. But you would not want to say as part of an acceptance speech, "Thank you very much. This is a great ornament." (Unless, of course, they gave you something to decorate a Christmas tree.)

What to Add:
Specifics. Everybody sees things differently. What you consider beautiful may be what someone else considers plain. What you think boring, others may find exciting. You need to be specific enough in your language to put in your reader's mind exactly what you want him or her to see. Using adjectives such as *pretty, beautiful, ugly, fun,* and *boring* doesn't cut it. You have to do more. If I tell you,

"The mountains in northern Spain are very beautiful," will you be able to describe those mountains to someone else? No. How could you? I haven't described them to you. You have to explain what you mean by giving details. Remember, your reader can read your work, not your mind.

Support. If you've made a statement that prompts the reader to ask, "How do you know?" you can add quotations from outside sources or include a personal experience for support. Using quotations from outside sources does not make you sound ignorant. In fact, it has the opposite effect. Giving credit to someone else for use of their words or ideas makes your writing appear substantial, especially if the person you quote is an expert in the field. Personal experiences have a similar effect. They give the reader reason to trust what you write.

You should develop your writing by including examples, comparisons, contrasts, metaphors, and analogies—anything that will help clarify your points and help your reader understand your ideas. I use examples in this chapter to show you what a wordy sentence looks like and how to improve it. Without those examples, you might read the paragraph and not really understand what I'm trying to say. You already know I am found of analogies. Find what works for you so you can make your writing clear, specific and detailed.

The Third Stage: An Outside Reader. Once you have shaped your paper to your satisfaction in the second revision stage by cutting, changing, and adding, you must allow someone else to read your work. This can be hard. When you write, you pour yourself unto the page. Handing "yourself" to a critical reader can feel like putting your neck on a chopping block. What if you fail? What if the reader doesn't like what you wrote? What if they actually suggest you change something?!

It's easier and less stressful, especially if you're writing for a class, to bypass the third stage of revision altogether. After all, the paper DOES look finished. You know what you're saying. You've spent a lot of time working on it. Why bother finding a reader?

Without an outside point of view, you have no idea how your writing will be perceived or understood. You can ask yourself Murray's questions all day long, but until you have a real reader, you don't know if you've succeeded in communicating your ideas. Don't be afraid to seek out a different perspective.

When you receive your reader's comments, you revise again. Readers have their own prejudices, their own ways of perceiving things, their own opinions, and their own hang-ups, so you have to decide which criticisms to accept and which to ignore. Be careful not to throw out criticisms because you're uncomfortable with the way they make you feel. Feeling hurt and/or defensive is normal.

You have to be able to work past those feelings and judge a reader's comments objectively. Also, never feel like a reader's criticisms are a personal attack. Unless you have a bad reader who makes inappropriate personal comments, his or her comments are directed toward your writing, not you.

Finding a good reader can be difficult. You don't need someone to tell you, "Sounds good to me." Such useless comments take the pressure off the reader and cheat the writer. A good reader shows you where your writing can improve and where your writing works. A good reader is specific. To recognize a good reader, you need to become a good reader. Chapter 10 shows you how.

10

THE PINK TUMMY OF WRITING

*Writing is hard work.
It's like being in a dark cave. You don't know where the walls are, the boundaries... You have to sense the limits of where you are, what you're doing and where you're going.*

—Arthur Miller

Writing a good paper is hard work. It's easy to write a paper the night before it's due because you can say, "Oh, I just pulled it off at the last minute." You take yourself off the hook by giving your writing an excuse to be poor. And especially if you get a decent grade out of last minute scribble, you're able to say "I didn't even spend any time on it"—meaning—"Think what I *could* have done if I had *tried*."

The fact is, a decent grade, even the highest grade, doesn't really mean anything. Does an A in a composition class mean the paper is publishable? That the writer is ready to take on Comp II? That the writer is the best in the class? Grades are a subjective and meaningless construction of the educational system. They cannot tell you if your writing is superior or not. I want you to learn to judge your own writing so you don't have to rely on grades to assess the quality of your work.

Critiquing another student's work will help you learn what to look for in good writing. You will learn what you like and what you don't like. You will see what works and what doesn't work. You will come to recognize confusing sentence structures and redundancies. You will see how good organization makes a paper easy to read and understand and how poor organization does the opposite.

Unless you learn what strengths and weaknesses to look for in a piece of writing, you will find it difficult to successfully revise anything you've written. Evaluating the work of someone else helps you become a good reader. By focusing your ability to think critically, you begin to do more than scan the words on a page. You begin to see how those words work together on both a small scale (one sentence) and a large scale (the whole paper). A good reader can point to areas that need improvement. The more you practice, the better you will be.

Critical thinking is not something new to you. You reason, evaluate evidence, and draw conclusions on a day-to-day basis. Every decision you make, no matter how small, is based on some type of reasoning. When you set your alarm for a certain time in the morning, you choose that time based on a number of factors: how long it takes you to get dressed, how long your drive is to work or school, if you eat breakfast, etc. You choose which streets and highways to take based on your knowledge of traffic patterns and the alternate routes possible to arrive at your destination. Everything you do is based on evidence of some sort.

You can already explain why you like one movie, but hate another. You can tell someone why you dress the way you do. You can tell someone why you feel comfortable or uncomfortable in certain situations or places such as museums, rock concerts, art galleries, or rave parties. Chances are, you already have an opinion about everything that goes on around you, and if you pushed yourself, you could explain your reasoning. The following questions can help you focus your critical abilities on a paper.

CRITICAL Q's

ORGANIZATION:

1. What is the main point of the paper?

2. Can you tell where the paper is going after reading the first or the first and second paragraphs?

3. Does the paper wander off topic? Where?

4. Does each paragraph elaborate on one, and only one, idea?

5. Can you follow the writer's logical progression from idea to idea? If not, explain why.

6. Where does the writer shift too abruptly from one idea to the next?

7. How does the conclusion wrap up the paper effectively?

INTEREST:

1. What catches your attention and makes you want to read the paper?
2. What keeps your attention and makes the paper interesting?
3. Where does your attention lag?
4. Which words or phrases do you find appealing? Why?
5. What images do you like? Why?
6. What do you want to know more about?
7. What would you rather hear less about?

CLARITY:

1. Where do you find the writer's words or ideas confusing? How are they confusing?
2. Do you have to read sentences twice to understand what the writer is saying? Where?
3. Are any words or phrases repeated? Which ones?
4. Which "broad" adjectives (like beautiful or boring) need to be clarified?
5. What needs to be CUT to improve both flow and clarity?

SUPPORT:

1. Could the paper use more detail? Where?
2. Does the writer need to use examples? Where?
3. Would personal experiences enhance the paper? Where?
4. Do claims in the paper need support from outside sources? Where?

OVERALL ASSESMENT:

1. Can you hear the voice of the writer? Can you pinpoint specific passages where the voice of the writer shines through?

2. How could the paper communicate with you, the reader, better?

3. What have you learned, if anything, from reading the paper? What have you seen from a new perspective?

When you receive one of your peer's papers to evaluate, you need to read the paper once or twice, without marking anything, to get a feel for what the writer is saying. Once you have an idea about what the writer is trying to do, read the paper again with the above questions in your mind and a pen in your hand. Mark places that will help you respond to the questions. Write comments in the margins. Circle words you like or don't like. Use stars or arrows or question marks—anything that will help you evaluate the paper.

When you finally write up your discoveries, you must be thorough and specific. Polite responses such as "sounds good to me" and "looks good" don't count. You need to point out specific areas that need improvement. Feel free to give suggestions about how the writer might change something to make it better, but keep in mind that the paper you are evaluating is not your paper. You have to help the writer with his writing, not rewrite the paper with your style.

If you are evaluating one of your peer's papers, chances are, one of your peer's is evaluating yours. So when you comment on a paper, remember that the writer has feelings capable of being hurt, just as you do. You don't want to be too nice, but you don't want to be too harsh either. You want to be straightforward and honest—helpful, not hurtful.

When you pour your heart into what you write, criticism can feel like a cold knife blade plunging into your chest. No one wants to put serious work into a paper only to have somebody (professor, friend, parent, acquaintance, stranger) say something negative. But learning to spend time writing a good paper and learning to accept criticism is part of the game. We all hope that people will read our work and say, "Wow! That's the best thing I've ever read!" That's okay, as long as we can accept NOT hearing those words and take a little criticism instead.

When you finally receive your critic's comments, keep the protective feelings you have for your paper in check. If you are defensive, your attitude will prevent you from using those comments to improve your writing. You don't have to agree with or use everything your critic suggests. And if you can be objective, you will find it easier to know what advice to accept, and what to ditch. To improve, we have to be willing to bare the vulnerable pink tummy of our writing. So roll over, and let the criticism begin.

11
IT TAKES ALL KINDS

Of the modes of persuasion furnished by the spoken word there are three kinds. The first kind depends on the personal character of the speaker; the second on putting the audience into a certain frame of mind; the third on the proof, provided by the words of the speech itself.

—*Aristotle*

If you have completed a critical evaluation of one of your classmate's papers, you know you already possess the critical thinking necessary to judge whether a piece of writing works or not. You know what you like and don't like. You can pinpoint sections of the paper you don't understand. Why should you go further? The more you learn about the make-up of writing, the more you hone your natural ability to critique.

You should realize by now that the goal of writing something that will be read is communication. Your purpose in writing and your audience will determine the form and style your writing takes, but regardless of what you wish to communicate, if your purpose or language is unclear, your reader will become confused and your will have failed to reach your goal.

For the purpose of this textbook, I place all writing in four categories: informative, narrative, personal, and persuasive. Since most of your academic writing will fall under the category of persuasive writing, I have chosen to leave that explanation for another chapter. For now, I want us to focus on the first three. When you can recognize how and where the following techniques will improve a piece of writing, you take your first step toward becoming a better writer.

INFORMATIVE WRITING

When you give directions, answer an essay question that requires you to supply facts, record the results of an experiment, explain how to perform a task, or take minutes for a meeting, you are writing primarily to convey information. Such writing does not have to be cold, boring, and impersonal, but it should be tight, direct, and factual. Save opinions, extended descriptions, and personal experiences for persuasive and narrative papers.

If you're getting directions to a party, you don't need to hear the entire story about the cop who pulled your friend over the last time he went to the same party. You might want to read, "When you cross the bridge, the speed limit becomes 35. Don't speed. The police enforce the speed limit on Gulf Breeze Hwy like the lions of the Serengeti stalking their prey." But you don't need to know how fast your friend was going when he was stopped, what he was wearing, how he felt, the cost of the ticket, or what he said when the officer asked for his license. You simply don't need that information; it just gets in the way. You want facts, not fluff.

The Summary. Summaries are useful when you need to provide your reader with information that is not common knowledge. You might need to explain the results of a court ruling, the characteristics of an African animal, or the procedure for entering a beauty contest. Regardless of what you need to relate, you must remember to make your summary "short and sweet." Otherwise, your reader will feel you have wandered from your topic and may lose interest.

When you begin using outside sources to support your writing, you may read ten or more (and later, fifty or more) articles during your research. At some point, they all begin to look the same. Summarizing can help you remember the difference between articles three and seven without having to go back and reread each one. Such a group of summaries is called an annotated bibliography.

Summaries can do more than help you with future papers. The amount of reading you have to do during a semester can seem overwhelming and discouraging, especially when you take the time to read an article, a book, or a chapter in a text only to wake up the next morning with the realization that you have no clue what you read, that most of the information went in one eye and out the other. Writing a summary immediately after you read something can help jar your memory and give you a good reference later. You will find your own way to summarize, but I have discovered two ways that work equally well.

Lump summary. Read through the entire piece, let your mind knead the information, and then sit down and write a brief summary of what you remember. Sometimes underlining passages while reading can help trigger your memory when you go back to summarize. This works best for short or sectioned works.

Spot summary. For those of you who find it difficult to concentrate for long periods, a spot summary can be the best way both to summarize and to focus your attention. Sitting at the computer, or with a notebook and pen in hand, summarize as you go, paragraph by paragraph. Then read over the notes you've written and condense them.

You may take exams with essay questions that require you to summarize what you have learned about a subject either as your sole response or as a basis for another response. Consider the following questions:

1. What are the arguments for and against capital punishment in the United States?
2. How have the theories of Descartes and Voltaire affected animal rights?

The first question requires you to simply regurgitate the information you have learned. The second question requires you to regurgitate the information and then respond to a question based on that information.

If you summarize your class reading and lecture notes, you will find yourself better prepared for exams, especially essay questions. And if you have to write papers based on your readings, you will have already put in words much of the information you need for those papers.

NARRATIVE WRITING

While students associate narrative writing—telling a story—with creative literature, writers can use narrative techniques to enhance persuasive papers. Through point-of-view, description, dialogue character development, and conflict, a good story can pull you into the plot and make you feel you are RIGHT THERE with the characters and that the things happening to those characters are happening RIGHT NOW. Whether you realize it or not, you are already familiar with these techniques from watching movies and reading novels. Let's take a closer look at how you can incorporate them into your writing.

Point of View. You can manipulate the way your reader perceives your writing by altering the "narrative" point of view—the perspective from which you are writing—and the "grammatical" point of view—the use of first, second, or third person.

The "narrative" point of view is a writer's approach to a subject. Consider the difference between the movies <u>Rush Hour</u> and <u>Ocean's 11</u>. In the first, the criminals are the villains. In the second, they are the heroes. The point of view determines where the audience's sympathy lies. In the same way, an argument for or against legalizing marijuana will change based on whether the author approaches the subject from a medical, political, religious, or philosophical perspective. If you are aware of your "narrative" point-of-view when writing, you will be able to anticipate your reader's reaction and use that reaction to deal with your topic more effectively.

The "grammatical" point-of-view is a writer's choice of pronouns, specifically I, you, or he/she. First-person narration—using I—generally makes the reader feel he is engaged on a personal level with the writer. Such closeness can often have a powerful impact on the reader.

I had to drop out of school because I lost my job.

Second-person narration—using you—directly addresses the reader by asking him to place himself in a situation or by telling him to do something. While using second person can encourage the reader to participate in your writing, such a direct approach can actually have the opposite effect, distancing the reader because he does not want to be forced into something.

Imagine you had to drop out of school because you lost your job.

Third person narration—using he/she—takes the writer out of the writing and does not actively reach out to the reader. Using third person narration is like trying to get a room full of people to listen to you by drawing their interest, not demanding their attention. It takes talent, effort, and perseverance.

Jennifer had to drop out of school because she lost her job.

Which point-of-view works best? Your writing must decide. If you're writing about the use of feminine imagery in Hemingway, you probably don't need or want to use first or second person. However, if you are trying to persuade your audience to try Yoga, a personal experience using first person might be useful. Keep in mind, though, that for a persuasive paper, using only personal experiences is not enough. If your sole support for claiming that Yoga can help heal a person spiritually is that you went to a few classes (or five years of classes), you don't have an adequate argument. But if you provide other support for such a claim, your own experience can be helpful.

*A note on formality: Many instructors believe that using *I* or *you* is too informal for academic papers. I disagree. But my professional opinion about the controversial *I* is beside the point. You should be aware that not all of your instructors will approve. So before you write a paper for a class, ask your professor how he or she feels about the use of *I*, and go from there.

Description. The person who reads what you write cannot read your mind, so you must be specific enough with your language to put in that person's head exactly what you want him to see. However, since everyone sees things differently, you must do more than TELL your reader what something or someone is like. You must SHOW him. As I wrote in Chapter 7, using broad adjectives such as *beautiful*, *ugly*, *fun*, or *boring* is not enough.

For instance, to write "English is boring" doesn't SHOW the reader HOW it is boring. If you can relate the feeling of boredom without mentioning the word *boring*, you've done your writing a favor: "The teacher spends half the class reading 'great' literature with a soft, monotonous tone. I have to fight to keep my eyes from closing."

You should also respect your reader enough to allow him to make his own decisions about what you are describing to him. Telling your reader, for instance, that "underage drinking is wrong" indicates that you doubt his ability to draw that conclusion from what you have written. In essence, you tell him that your ideas cannot stand on their own. You have to trust your writing to relate your message, not your statements.

Dialogue. Without realistic and interesting dialogue, a movie can quickly become tedious and boring. Think of dialogue as "active" language. When you include dialogue in your writing, you give your reader a chance to hear somebody speaking. Many narrative techniques such as character development, description, and point-of-view are created through dialogue. Whether you use quotations from an interview or you create a conversation to make a point, you can include dialogue in your writing to give life to an experience you are trying to relate.

Character Development. Stephen King is a master of character development and uses it "against" his readers. He often elaborates on a character's personality, feelings, and thoughts until we, as readers, are emotionally involved—then he kills off the character in the next chapter. King uses our connection with the character, which he creates through description, to surprise us, to manipulate our reaction.

You can manipulate the reaction of your readers by choosing what to make "come alive." If you are writing about electrical lines causing cancer in neighborhoods, you want your reader to do more than say, "That's a shame." You want him to see those people as his own family members. And if you are writing about animal abuse in zoos, you want your reader to feel more than just sympathy; you want him to experience what those animals are feeling. Only when you stir your reader's emotions can you effect change.

Conflict. Conflict makes us invest our emotions in a story and holds our interest. We want to know how the innocent man will escape wrongful imprisonment, how the kidnapped child will be rescued, or how the wife deals with her husband's infidelity. A paper works the same way. If you don't build up enough tension, your writing will be flat and your point, dull. Create conflict and your reader will WANT to see where you're going and what the outcome will be.

Part of creating conflict is establishing your purpose (point or thesis) in writing. If you do not feel a story has a purpose, you will lose interest and wonder why you're wasting your time. Cindy Wine, my childhood friend, teases me constantly because I loved the movie *A Thin Red Line* and she saw it as "a bunch of men wading through grass." If your reader doesn't see a point to your writing, he will stop reading—Cindy left the theater.

PERSONAL WRITING

Whether you are writing in a journal, composing a letter, or developing a creative non-fiction piece from your own experiences, personal writing can be a wonderful outlet for emotions and can help us make decisions by clarifying our thoughts. For university courses, however, personal writing is not enough. Your writing must have a point beyond self-reflection.

You can use personal experiences to enhance your writing, but if you have no message in mind when you write, you can trust that your reader will have a difficult time figuring out what they are reading and why. You don't want your reader to feel he has wasted his time—that there was no point—but random thoughts and miscellaneous experiences can do just that. Personal experiences are best used to enhance a paper, not as the sole focus of your writing.

As we move on to the next chapter on persuasive writing, keep in mind that the boundaries between these categories are not firm. Narrative writing can be personal. Informative writing can be narrative. And persuasive writing can include informative, narrative, and personal techniques. I use these categories for one reason only: so you can learn to recognize when a particular form of writing might improve a piece of writing. But my explanations are merely a guide. Only you can decide how you want mix the different forms I have shown you or where to use them in your writing.

12

PERSUASIVE AWARENESS

The secret of all good writing is sound judgment.

—Horace

By now, I'm sure some of you are fed up with talk of writing and revision. You're certain you'll never use the stuff. After all, you're getting a B.S. in Computer Science. However, contrary to what you, and many students like you, may think, writing is not just an "English major thing." You can use writing for so much more than evaluating literature or expressing creativity. You can use writing to develop a solution to a problem, convince a reader that your perspective on an issue is correct, illustrate a new way of looking at a subject, or help someone with a problem by giving advice. And regardless of your major, most university courses require that you write papers which present arguments based on evidence—persuasive papers.

You might have to prove that the Jews were blamed for the Black Plague, that people with schizophrenia should not be imprisoned for murder, that the infomercial is an effective form of advertising, that the programming language C++ fails to retain the efficiency of the older version C, or that public schools should review their policies regarding mainstreaming. No matter the subject, your ability to think critically and write persuasively will determine your success or failure.

As I told you in Chapter 10, you already have natural critical instincts. You know what you like and don't like, and you can explain why. Writing persuasively relies on your natural ability to argue and present logical points. We "argue" all the time. As young children, we give our parents reasons to allow us certain privileges. Perhaps they even set up those reasons for us. "You can't play with your friends until you clean up your room." Okay. Reversed, that statement provides a logical argument. "Mom and Dad, I have cleaned up my room; therefore, I should be allowed to go out with my friends."

When you combine your ability to argue with awareness and research, you have the makings of a great paper. While arguing may come quite naturally to you, most students need to hone their skills of awareness and learn how to adequately research a topic.

If you are not constantly AWARE of how you are making your reader feel, you risk loosing his interest and his respect. As with critical thinking and the ability to argue, awareness is nothing new to you. When you hold a conversation, you have learned to judge what you say by watching your listener's body language. If, for instance, you tell your girlfriend that your new neighbor is "dropdead gorgeous" and she gives you the silent treatment for the next week, you make an important connection. You realize that by mentioning another girl's beauty you make her feel insecure. So the next time you're face with a similar situation, you might tell her another woman is "nice" and leave off a comment about her looks. And if your girlfriend asks you, "Is she pretty?" You learn to say, "She's okay" or "Not as pretty as you."

Writing is more difficult because you don't have a second chance to change your language. You have to anticipate the feelings of your reader before you write. An outside reader can help you see where you can make something more palatable for a reader, but you need to learn to put yourself in the reader's place and ask yourself how what you're reading would make you feel. Developing this empathic ability will help you in any type of situation, but it is especially helpful when you take on a controversial issue in your writing.

When you argue a point with two clearly defined sides, your reader may come to your work with his defenses already up. You want to anticipate those readers' reactions so you don't push them further away. You don't need to convince the people who already agree with you, you need to convince the people who disagree with you. So you have to present your argument in a way that will not only compel your opponents to read what you've written, but may also change their opinions.

If, for instance, you want to convince your readers that U.S. citizens should not be allowed to own firearms, you don't want to offend the very people you are trying to convince by inferring (or stating outright) that NRA members are gunwielding, murdering imbeciles. And if you want to convince your readers that U.S. citizens have the right to own guns, you don't want to infer that people who are for gun control are ignorant, spineless fascists.

To be able to deal with readers who come to your writing already disagreeing with you, you need to know the opposing argument as well as (or even better) than you know your own. If you are familiar with both sides, you can often use the opposing viewpoint in your favor. Think of persuasive writing as a bout of fencing—if you cannot anticipate your opponent's moves, you will lose.

But knowing the opposing argument is not enough. You must also gain the attention and the respect of your reader by being AWARE of what you are saying. If you make general statements that you have no way to support, or you stereotype groups, or you use words that have different meanings depending on whom you ask, your readers will lose respect for you, and you will lose any chance you have of convincing them of anything. In fact, what your readers will think is, "What an idiot!"

For example, to say "feminists are against family" makes too many assumptions. For one thing, what exactly is a feminist? Does that word mean the same thing to you as it does to someone else? I know people who argue that feminists are power-hungry male haters. But I also know people who see feminists as women who feel they deserve the right to vote. And what constitutes "family"? A mother and father? A single parent? Grandparents? Friends? The following is a list of common fallacies you should be able to recognize and avoid in your writing.

Hasty generalization: generalizing from inadequate evidence; stereotyping is hasty generalization using prejudiced claims about a group of people.
False analogy: using a comparison in which the differences outweigh the similarities or in which the similarities are irrelevant to the claim the analogy is intended to support.
Begging the question: using a kind of circular reasoning that offers as proof of an argument a version of the argument itself or using a presumably shared assumption to stand for proof.
Irrelevant argument: reaching a conclusion that does not follow from the premises.
False cause: assuming that because two events are related in time, the first caused the second. Coincidence.
Self-contradiction: using two premises that cannot both be true
Red Herring: sidetracking the issue by raising a second, unrelated issue.
Guilt by association: attacking a person's ideas because of the person's interests or associates.
Jumping on the bandwagon: implying that something is right or is permissible because "everyone is doing it."
False or irrelevant authority: citing the opinion of a person who has no expertise about the subject.
Card-stacking: ignoring evidence on the other side of a question.
Either-or-fallacy: offering only two alternatives when more exist.

Taking something out of context: distorting an idea or a fact by separating it from the material surrounding it.
Appeal to ignorance: assuming that an argument is valid simply because there is no evidence on the other side of the issue.
Ambiguity: using expressions that are not clear because they have more than one meaning.
Non Sequitur: draws unwarranted conclusions from seemingly ample evidence.
Circular argument: supports a question by restating it.
Fears of Audience: appeal of this sort arouses an emotional response by playing on the irrational fears and prejudices of the audience. Communists, fascists, tree-huggers, welfare babies, crack heads, etc.

Awareness also means understanding that not everyone sees things the way you see them. People carry different perspectives of life around depending on where they were born, how they were raised, the friends they had growing up, the friends they have now, their religion, their sexual orientation, their job, their pay, etc. Knowing who your readers are, the specific people for whom you are writing, will help you know how to argue your points.

Regardless of what you are writing about, you have a specific audience in mind whether you realize it or not. And rarely is that audience a "general" audience. If you are writing about educational reforms, your target audience is not a group of doctors. If you are writing about new computer advances, you're not writing for people who know nothing about computers. And if you are writing about the benefits of a university degree, you're not writing for retirees or people who already have graduated.

Few things are directed to a general audience. Think about it. Name any movie you choose. Then start crossing off the groups that the movie was NOT intended for. Start paying attention to the commercials on television. Which audience are they targeting? Which commercials appeal to you, and why?

Knowing your audience helps you direct your language. Clearly, papers you write for a university class have an obvious audience: your instructor. But push yourself to go further. Find a way to direct your writing so that your papers seem less like boring academic dribble and more like active, interested participation. Each discipline has a "conversation" going on. Professors and researchers "talk" to each other through the articles they publish. When you try to include yourself in that ongoing conversation, your professors WILL notice. I cannot express the difference between a paper written to barely meet the requirements and a paper struggling to say something worth reading. Before you write a paper for a certain course, find journal articles in that discipline and see what the writers are saying and how they are saying it; then write accordingly.

Awareness in writing includes even more than knowing what you're saying, directing your message to an audience, and anticipating how your reader will interpret your words. Awareness also means recognizing the quirks of your writing and knowing when they work and when they don't.

Just as we develop habits of conversation, we develop habits of writing, our personal style. And you don't have to write for thirty years to have a recognizable style. At this stage in the semester, I would bet money that you could write a paper, leave off your name, and your instructor would know that it belonged to you. Especially when students have a powerful voice behind their unique style, the origin of their work is unquestionable.

Certain habits of writing, however, can detract from our message, just as habits of conversation can frustrate our listeners. When I verbally tell a story, I have a tendency to begin with questions and information that make my listener wait to know what I am talking about. I could, for instance, easily begin a conversation like this:

> This may say something about the type of person I am, or the type of person I want to be. And I don't know what possessed me to walk in the store. Did I really think that eggs were that important? I don't even remember why I left the house in the first place, considering the rain. But I don't think normal people react the way I do when confronted.

I can go on and on and on before getting to what I want to say. It's not a good habit. In fact, it's a very bad habit, and my friends often exclaim with exasperation, "Okay, okay! Just tell us what happened!"

You should get to know your own quirky habits and biases so you can catch them on paper and go to work with the scalpel. Often, we are unable to "see" these peculiar habits in our own writing, which makes an outside reader indispensable. Just as we can find places that need to be cut in other people's work, they can find them in ours.

To be constantly aware of how and what you are writing is probably the most important skill you can learn. And part of being aware is knowing when you need to support your claims with source material—with research. Chapter 13 will help you learn how to find material that will give your arguments support and credibility and will show you how to include that material in your writing.

13

THE RESEARCH PAPER

*What is written without effort
is in general read without pleasure.*

—Samuel Johnson

For reasons I have yet to understand, students who can churn out a personal essay with the expertise of a NASA scientist turn to quivering mush when asked to write a research paper. And no matter what their instructors say, those piles of quivering mush refuse to believe they can translate their talents for personal drama into the research arena. Their voices, which once blasted through the page, become so consciously bound that all personality behind their message dies, leaving behind hollow words connecting strings of quotations in a futile effort to sound "academic."

The fact is, nothing about writing changes when you write a research paper. The process is the same. The same rules apply for introductions and conclusions. You move through the same stages of revision. You still need to know your audience. You still have to form your own ideas and make your own connections. Writing a research paper simply means you support the claims you make in your writing with evidence.

A research paper is NOT what many students think of as a "report." From elementary school through high school, students write reports in which they find information about a subject and reiterate that information in paper format. Young students need to know how to find information, and they need to learn how to put that information in their own words, but such report writing is the equivalent of learning the ABC's before learning to read; it's a fundamental step, not the ultimate goal.

As a university student, you need to say good-bye to the "report." You must now develop your own opinions, make your own assumptions, and propose your own solutions. Don't merely reiterate what others have said and done; instead, use their work to prove YOUR points and support YOUR conclusions. Have confidence that YOU have something worthwhile to contribute. You can learn a lot from doing research, but you should have the attitude that others have a lot to learn from your ideas.

Finding a Research Topic: Too many students think research topics have to be cold and uninteresting. Not true. You can find support for almost any topic you want to write on. You can even turn a personal paper into a research paper if you can find, within your personal experience, a message you wish to communicate to a specific audience.

I had a student one semester who discovered, after working through the "thirteen things" of chapter five, that she wanted to write about her cheerleading experience in high school. Of course, when she thought about trying to find research, her immediate reaction was, "I guess I should choose another topic."

After some thought, though, she decided that part of what she wanted to discuss was that cheerleading was not considered a sport in her high school, but rather a club, and the distinction affected the amount of funding the cheerleading team received. She was then able to find a number of articles from cheerleading magazines, which discussed how cheerleading has become a sport, as well as the funding reports from her high school's athletic department.

If you have a general idea about what you want to write, but you have not narrowed your idea to a specific topic, you can do a little preliminary research to see what's out there. By looking for pathways that spark your interest, research can help you form a concrete topic. Doing this preliminary research can also help you discover what topics haven't been discussed and what needs attention.

Doing Research: Eventually, all resources will be available via computer. You can already find numerous books, journals, and newspapers online and more appear everyday, but the majority of potential resources have not found their way to the information highway. You still need to be able to find a book or article in the library and go through the motions of checking out a book or copying what you want to read.

Since all libraries are a little different, you should find out when you can attend a library orientation and get to know the services they provide. Even if everything you need is available on the Internet, your librarian can show you the best way to find those Internet sources and can help steer you away from potentially unreliable information.

With home access to the Internet, research seems easy and a trip to the library can feel like a waste of time. You think, "Hey, I'll just plug my topic into Yahoo and see what pops up." However, while searching through Yahoo can bring up excellent, reliable sites, it will unfortunately bring up those that are not so reliable. ANYONE, regardless of credentials, can post ANYTHING, regardless of accuracy, on the web. I discovered today that even information which appears connected with a university may not be trustworthy.

I searched for *Holocaust* with Google and found a site apparently from the University of Texas at Austin which included the following information:

> The "Holocaust" is the biggest propaganda coup ever fabricated. It is a lie. The reason the "Holocaust" was created was to prevent ANY and all criticism of the Jewish theft of Palestine in the creation of Israel.
> <http://www.cwrl.utexas.edu/~syverson/309-spring96/studentwork/project1/curtiss/THE_HOLOCAUST_NEVER_HA_377.html>

So, be careful. Something as obvious as a Holocaust denial is easy to spot. But for subjects you know nothing about, it is much more difficult to determine if the information you are reading is legitimate or not. As a rule, never use anything off the web unless you can find an author and that author's credentials as well as the publishing information for what you are reading. No author was listed for the above writing, and no publication information was made available.

Most professors have already explored their subjects on the web and they know which sites are useful and reliable. So you can ask them if there are sites on the web which will help supplement the class material. If you find a site you want to use, you can ask your instructor if the site is legitimate. If, however, you begin your research at your library's homepage, you will inevitably find better sources to work with and spend less time trying to sort through and evaluate the endless material on the World Wide Web.

Including Research: There are two main ways you can include source material in your writing. You can put an author's exact words in quotations marks, or you can paraphrase—put in your own words what someone else has written

Think of paraphrasing as a form of translation. If you translate one of García Lorca's poems into English, it doesn't become your poem. You may be the translator, but you are not the author. When you paraphrase, you translate. You use different words to say the same thing. But using different words doesn't make you the author. I suggest that you forget about paraphrasing and always use quotations. It's too easy to fall into the plagiarism trap when you rewrite something in your own words.

Plagiarism means using someone else's words or ideas without giving that person credit. Plagiarism is not limited to published material, and includes lecture notes, other students' papers, and even papers you have written for other classes.

Yes, you can plagiarize yourself. If a student is caught plagiarizing, he usually fails much more than the assignment: he fails the entire course. Students can even be suspended or expelled from their university for committing plagiarism. I cannot stress the importance of this issue. Do not take any chances. If you use someone else's ideas or words, please give that person credit.

Contrary to what some students think, using quotations in your writing and giving credit for ideas does not make your writing appear weak. Rather, when you acknowledge source material, your writing seems strong and grounded. There's a fine line, however, between using too much and not using enough. Using too many quotations and paraphrasing too much makes your paper seem like a meaningless string of other people's ideas. Not using enough makes your paper look unsupported.

For publishing purposes, each discipline has its own paper format and specific rules for citing quoted material. English departments use MLA (Modern Language Association) documentation. Appendix A contains a demonstration of MLA format in which I discuss methods for including quotations and citing quoted material.

Even though there are strict rules for paper format and policies against plagiarism, and even though finding material to support your writing can take a lot of time and energy, research writing can be fun. Finding the material you need to support your writing is like going on a treasure hunt. And discovering where a quote will fit perfectly within your own words is like putting a puzzle together. Remember, you don't have to change your writing style to participate in the academic community. Change instead your perception of what *academic* means, and let the rest take care of itself.

Conclusion
I HATE WRITING

Scott took LITERATURE so solemnly.
He never understood that it was just writing
as well as you can and finishing what you start.

—Ernest Hemingway
(about F. Scott Fitzgerald)

"I hate writing." I know I have felt this way more than once in my life. I wonder how many of you have felt the same way too. But why? What is there to hate about picking up a pen and pouring out our thoughts? Well, I know the answer for me—"because it's hard!" And writing—GOOD writing—is hard and can be the most emotionally, mentally (and physically if you are attempting to pick up the computer and throw it in the trash) draining and difficult work there is.

Sometimes there are other reasons that we decide to hate writing or to say, "I can't write." It doesn't take a weak soul to be discouraged by a teacher who returns a paper bleeding to death with red marks, demanding that we change our words or structure in ways we don't really understand. Try not to let those experiences, if you've had them, keep you from becoming the best writer you can be.

I had a good friend in an English graduate program (no names this time). The head of the department told her that she couldn't write, that she wouldn't make it through the program, that she would never succeed. He actually said these things to her. But my friend pushed on. Now she's working on her Ph.D. She has given papers at conferences. And she is working toward the publication of a book. I'd say she's pretty darn successful.

In this textbook, I've given you a few tools to help your writing, and I've given you the basics of becoming a good reader. You have to take it from there. I refuse to give you a fill-in-the-blank pattern for churning out a paper. It's easy to imitate a pattern. Easy. It's easy to say, "Your paper should have five paragraphs: an introduction, three supporting paragraphs, and a conclusion. And each paragraph should have three sentences." I want much more from you than that.

I want you to think, to create. I want you to manipulate the language. Play with new styles. Toy with new ideas. I want you to believe, to KNOW, that you have something to contribute. I want you to do the hardest thing there is: I want you to become writers. Once you discover what you can do with writing, you may just discover yourself.

0-595-34943-9

Printed in the United States
86290LV00005B/253-258/A